Syrup Recipes for Coffee and Tea

By

Brenda Van Niekerk

Copyright © 2013 Brenda Van Niekerk
All rights reserved.
Second Edition 2017

ISBN-13:978-1508965718
ISBN-10:1508965714

Content

Almond Syrup 1
Amaretto Syrup 4
Blackcurrant Syrup 6
Brandy Coffee Syrup 8
Caramel Cream Syrup 10
Caramel Syrup 12
Cardamom Coffee Syrup 14
Cherry Syrup 16
Chocolate Cherry Syrup 18
Chocolate Cream Syrup 20
Chocolate Hazelnut Syrup 22
Chocolate Peppermint Syrup 24
Chocolate Syrup 26
Cinnamon Syrup 28
Citrus Syrup 30
Coconut Syrup 32
Coffee Syrup 34
Cranberry Syrup 36
Gingerbread Syrup 38
Gooseberry Syrup 40
Granadilla Syrup 42
Hazelnut Syrup 44
Kahlua Coffee Syrup 46
Lavender Syrup 48
Lemon Ginger Syrup 50
Lemon Syrup 52

Lemongrass Syrup 54
Lime Syrup..56
Mexican Coffee Syrup 58
Mint Syrup..60
Mocha Syrup 62
Orange Syrup 64
Peppermint Syrup 66
Pumpkin Pie Syrup 68
Raspberry Syrup 70
Rose Honey Syrup 72
Rose Syrup..74
Saffron Honey Syrup 76
Saffron Syrup..78
Strawberry Syrup 80
Turkish Coffee Syrup 82
Vanilla Syrup 84

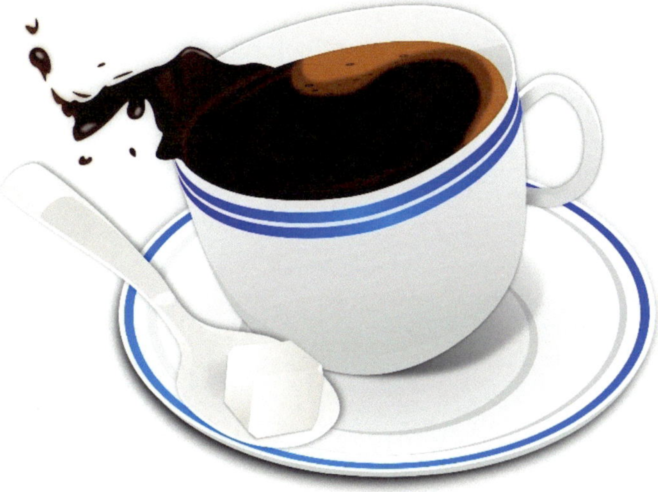

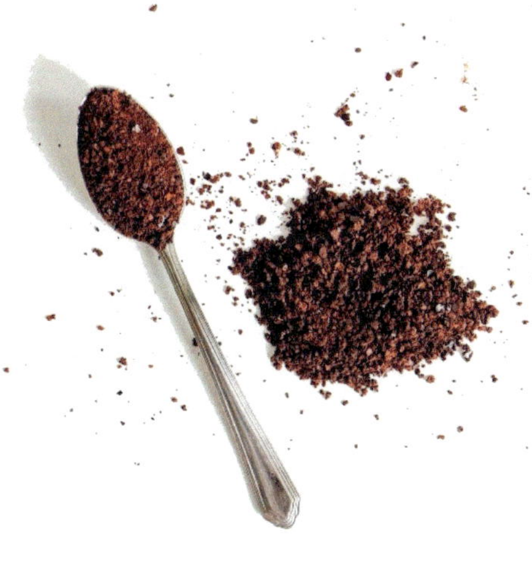

Almond Syrup

Ingredients

500 ml water

500 ml brown sugar

10 ml almond extract

Method

Combine the water, brown sugar and almond extract together in a saucepan.

Heat the mixture until the sugar has dissolved.

Stir occasionally.

Reduce the heat once the sugar has dissolved and simmer for 15 minutes.

Remove the syrup from the heat.

Allow the syrup to cool and the store in the refrigerator.

The syrup can be stored in the refrigerator for about a month.

Amaretto Syrup

Ingredients

500 ml water

500 ml sugar

37,5 ml Amaretto

Method

Combine the water and sugar together in a saucepan.

Heat the mixture until the sugar has dissolved.

Stir occasionally.

Reduce the heat once the sugar has dissolved and simmer for 15 minutes.

Remove the syrup from the heat.

Add the Amaretto.

Mix well.

Allow the syrup to cool and the store in the refrigerator.

The syrup can be stored in the refrigerator for about a month.

Blackcurrant Syrup

Ingredients

500 ml water

150 g sugar

200 g blackcurrants

Method

Wash the blackcurrants in cool water.

Place blackcurrants, sugar and water into a saucepan and bring to a boil.

Simmer and cook for 5 minutes.

Remove from the heat.

Pour the syrup through a strainer to remove the solids.

Allow the syrup to cool and the store in the refrigerator.

The syrup can be stored in the refrigerator for about a month.

Brandy Coffee Syrup

Ingredients

    500 ml sugar

    166 ml water

    333 ml strong black coffee

    125 ml brandy

Method

Combine the sugar and water together in a saucepan.

Heat the mixture until the sugar has dissolved.

Stir occasionally.

Remove the syrup from the heat once the sugar has dissolved.

Add the coffee and brandy

Allow the syrup to cool and the store in the refrigerator.

The syrup can be stored in the refrigerator for about a month.

Caramel Cream Syrup

Ingredients

250 ml unsalted butter (melted)

332 ml brown sugar

250 ml heavy cream

15 ml vanilla extract

Method

Combine the melted butter and brown sugar together in a saucepan.

Stir until the sugar dissolves.

Bring to the boil and cook for 1 minute.

Remove from the heat.

Add the cream and vanilla extract.

Mix well.

Allow the syrup to cool and the store in the refrigerator.

Caramel Syrup

Ingredients

500 ml water

500 ml sugar

83 ml dark brown sugar

1 vanilla bean (split lengthwise – scrape seeds out of pod)

10 ml vanilla extract

Method

Combine the white sugar, water, brown sugar and vanilla pod together in a saucepan.

Heat the mixture until the sugar has dissolved.

Stir occasionally.

Reduce the heat once the sugar has dissolved and simmer for 15 minutes.

Remove the syrup from the heat.

Remove the vanilla pod.

Add the vanilla extract.

Allow the syrup to cool and the store in the refrigerator.

The syrup can be stored in the refrigerator for about a month.

Cardamom Coffee Syrup

Ingredients

500 ml water

500 ml sugar

18 ml instant coffee granules

3 ml ground cardamom

2 ml saffron threads (packed)

12,5 ml rose water

Method

Combine the water, sugar, coffee granules, cardamom, saffron threads and rose water together in a saucepan.

Heat the mixture until the sugar has dissolved.

Stir occasionally.

Reduce the heat once the sugar has dissolved and simmer for 15 minutes.

Remove the syrup from the heat.

Allow the syrup to cool and the store in the refrigerator.

The syrup can be stored in the refrigerator for about a month.

Cherry Syrup

Ingredients

750 ml water

375 ml sugar

1 ½ lb cherries (pitted)

Method

Combine the sugar, water and cherries together in a saucepan.

Heat the mixture until the sugar has dissolved.

Stir occasionally.

Reduce the heat once the sugar has dissolved and simmer for 15 minutes.

Remove the syrup from the heat.

Pour the syrup through a strainer to remove the solids.

Allow the syrup to cool and the store in the refrigerator.

The syrup can be stored in the refrigerator for about a month.

Chocolate Cherry Syrup

Ingredients

550 ml sugar

250 ml unsweetened cocoa powder

500 ml water

10 ml cherry extract

Method

Combine the sugar, water, cocoa powder and cherry extract together in a saucepan.

Heat the mixture until the sugar has dissolved.

Stir occasionally.

Reduce the heat once the sugar has dissolved and simmer for 15 minutes.

Remove the syrup from the heat.

Allow the syrup to cool and the store in the refrigerator.

The syrup can be stored in the refrigerator for about a month.

Chocolate Cream Syrup

Ingredients

300 ml cream

150 g butter

225 g sugar

100 g milk chocolate (broken into pieced)

Method

Combine cream, butter and sugar in a saucepan.

Bring to boiling point and boil for 3 minutes.

Remove from heat and stir in the chocolate.

Stir until chocolate has melted.

Allow the syrup to cool and the store in the refrigerator.

The syrup can be stored in the refrigerator.

Chocolate Hazelnut Syrup

Ingredients

550 ml sugar

250 ml unsweetened cocoa powder

500 ml water

375 ml hazelnuts (finely chopped)

Method

Combine the sugar, water, cocoa powder and hazelnuts together in a saucepan.

Heat the mixture until the sugar has dissolved.

Stir occasionally.

Reduce the heat once the sugar has dissolved and simmer for 15 minutes.

Remove the syrup from the heat.

Pour the syrup through a strainer to remove the solids.

Allow the syrup to cool and the store in the refrigerator.

The syrup can be stored in the refrigerator for about a month.

Chocolate Peppermint Syrup

Ingredients

550 ml sugar

250 ml unsweetened cocoa powder

500 ml water

10 ml peppermint extract

Method

Combine the sugar, water, cocoa powder and peppermint extract together in a saucepan.

Heat the mixture until the sugar has dissolved.

Stir occasionally.

Reduce the heat once the sugar has dissolved and simmer for 15 minutes.

Remove the syrup from the heat.

Allow the syrup to cool and the store in the refrigerator.

The syrup can be stored in the refrigerator for about a month.

Chocolate Syrup

Ingredients

550 ml sugar

250 ml unsweetened cocoa powder

500 ml water

10 ml vanilla extract

Method

Combine the sugar, water, cocoa powder and vanilla extract together in a saucepan.

Heat the mixture until the sugar has dissolved.

Stir occasionally.

Reduce the heat once the sugar has dissolved and simmer for 15 minutes.

Remove the syrup from the heat.

Allow the syrup to cool and the store in the refrigerator.

The syrup can be stored in the refrigerator for about a month.

Cinnamon Syrup

Ingredients

500 ml soft brown water

500 ml water

5 ml ground cinnamon

Method

Combine the water, soft brown sugar and cinnamon together in a saucepan.

Heat the mixture until the sugar has dissolved.

Stir occasionally.

Reduce the heat once the sugar has dissolved and simmer for 15 minutes.

Remove the syrup from the heat.

Allow the syrup to cool and the store in the refrigerator.

The syrup can be stored in the refrigerator for about a month.

Citrus Syrup

Ingredients

Juice from 3 oranges

Juice from 3 lemons

Zest from 2 oranges

Zest from 2 lemons

750 ml boiling water

750 ml sugar

7,5 g Epsom salt

Method

Combine the orange juice, lemon juice, orange zest and lemon zest together.

Add the boiling water.

Leave the mixture to stand for 10 minutes.

Pour the syrup through a strainer to remove the solids.

Add the sugar and Epsom salt to the warm orange/ lemon juice mixture.

Stir until the sugar has dissolved.

Allow the syrup to cool and the store in the refrigerator.

The syrup can be stored in the refrigerator for about a month.

Coconut Syrup

Ingredients

500 ml water

500 ml water

10 ml coconut extract

Method

Combine the water, sugar and coconut extract together in a saucepan.

Heat the mixture until the sugar has dissolved.

Stir occasionally.

Reduce the heat once the sugar has dissolved and simmer for 15 minutes.

Remove the syrup from the heat.

Allow the syrup to cool and the store in the refrigerator.

The syrup can be stored in the refrigerator for about a month.

Coffee Syrup

Ingredients

750 ml strong extra black coffee

250 ml sugar

5 ml vanilla extract

Method

Combine the coffee, sugar and vanilla extract together in a saucepan.

Heat the mixture until the sugar has dissolved.

Stir occasionally.

Reduce the heat once the sugar has dissolved and simmer for 15 minutes.

Remove the syrup from the heat.

Allow the syrup to cool and the store in the refrigerator.

The syrup can be stored in the refrigerator for about a month.

Cranberry Syrup

Ingredients

500 ml sugar

500 ml water

375 ml fresh cranberries

Method

Combine the sugar, water and cranberries together in a saucepan.

Heat the mixture until the sugar has dissolved.

Stir occasionally.

Reduce the heat once the sugar has dissolved and simmer for 15 minutes.

Remove the syrup from the heat.

Pour the syrup through a strainer to remove the solids.

Allow the syrup to cool and the store in the refrigerator.

The syrup can be stored in the refrigerator for about a month.

Gingerbread Syrup

Ingredients

500 ml water

500 ml sugar

12,5 ml ground ginger

3 ml ground cinnamon

3 ml vanilla extract

Method

Combine the sugar, water, ginger, cinnamon and vanilla extract together in a saucepan.

Heat the mixture until the sugar has dissolved.

Stir occasionally.

Reduce the heat once the sugar has dissolved and simmer for 15 minutes.

Remove the syrup from the heat.

Allow the syrup to cool and the store in the refrigerator.

The syrup can be stored in the refrigerator for about a month.

Gooseberry Syrup

Ingredients

500 ml sugar

750 ml water

50 ml citric acid

1000 g gooseberries

Method

Combine the sugar, water, citric acid and gooseberries together in a saucepan.

Heat the mixture until the sugar has dissolved.

Stir occasionally.

Reduce the heat once the sugar has dissolved and simmer for 15 minutes.

Remove the syrup from the heat.

Pour the syrup through a strainer to remove the solids.

Allow the syrup to cool and the store in the refrigerator.

The syrup can be stored in the refrigerator for about a month.

Granadilla Syrup

Ingredients

500 ml sugar

375 ml boiling water

125 ml granadilla juice

3,5 ml Epsom salt

3,5 ml tartaric acid

Method

Combine the sugar, boiling water and granadilla juice together in a saucepan.

Stir until the sugar has dissolved.

Heat the mixture to boiling point.

Remove from the heat.

Pour the syrup through a strainer to remove the solids.

Add the Epsom salt and tartaric acid.

Mix well.

Allow the syrup to cool and the store in the refrigerator.

The syrup can be stored in the refrigerator for about a month.

Hazelnut Syrup

Ingredients

374 ml hazelnuts (chopped finely)

50 ml butter

374 ml maple syrup

Method

Combine the hazelnuts and butter together in a saucepan.

Cook the mixture until the hazelnuts turn brown.

Stir occasionally.

Add the maple syrup.

Mix well.

Heat the mixture but do not boil.

Pour the syrup through a strainer to remove the solids.

Allow the syrup to cool and the store in the refrigerator.

The syrup can be stored in the refrigerator for about 2 months.

Kahlua Coffee Syrup

Ingredients

500 ml water

500 ml sugar

50 ml Kahlua

25 ml espresso granules

Method

Combine the sugar, water, Kahlua and espresso granules together in a saucepan.

Heat the mixture until the sugar has dissolved.

Stir occasionally.

Reduce the heat once the sugar has dissolved and simmer for 15 minutes.

Remove the syrup from the heat.

Allow the syrup to cool and the store in the refrigerator.

The syrup can be stored in the refrigerator for about a month.

Lavender Syrup

Ingredients

500 ml sugar

500 ml water

62,5 ml lavender blossoms

Method

Combine the sugar, water and lavender blossoms together in a saucepan.

Heat the mixture until the sugar has dissolved.

Stir occasionally.

Reduce the heat once the sugar has dissolved and simmer for 15 minutes.

Remove the syrup from the heat.

Pour the syrup through a strainer to remove the solids.

Allow the syrup to cool and the store in the refrigerator.

The syrup can be stored in the refrigerator for about a month.

Lemon Ginger Syrup

Ingredients

500 ml sugar

250 ml water

250 ml lemon juice

12,5 ml ground ginger

Method

Combine the sugar, water, ginger and lemon juice together in a saucepan.

Heat the mixture until the sugar has dissolved.

Stir occasionally.

Reduce the heat once the sugar has dissolved and simmer for 15 minutes.

Remove the syrup from the heat.

Allow the syrup to cool and the store in the refrigerator.

The syrup can be stored in the refrigerator for about a month.

Lemon Syrup

Ingredients

500 ml sugar

250 ml water

250 ml lemon juice

Zest of 1 lemon

Method

Combine the sugar, water, lemon zest and lemon juice together in a saucepan.

Heat the mixture until the sugar has dissolved.

Stir occasionally.

Reduce the heat once the sugar has dissolved and simmer for 15 minutes.

Remove the syrup from the heat.

Allow the syrup to cool and the store in the refrigerator.

The syrup can be stored in the refrigerator for about a month.

Lemongrass Syrup

Ingredients

3 lemongrass stems (tops chopped off and bruised)

Fresh root ginger (about 5 cm and peeled and thinly sliced)

450 g sugar

600 ml water

Juice of 3 lemons

Method

Place the lemongrass and ginger into a saucepan.

Stir until the sugar has dissolved on a low heat.

Raise the heat and simmer for about 5 minutes.

Remove from the heat.

Add the lemon juice.

Pour the syrup through a strainer to remove the solids.

Allow the syrup to cool and the store in the refrigerator.

The syrup can be stored in the refrigerator for about a month.

Lime Syrup

Ingredients

Zest from 3 limes

Lime juice from 3 limes

750 g sugar

500 ml boiling water

6 ml tartaric acid

Method

Combine the lime zest, tartaric acid, sugar and boiling water.

Mix well to dissolve the sugar.

Add the limejuice and mix through.

Leave to stand overnight.

Pour the syrup through a strainer to remove the solids.

Allow the syrup to cool and the store in the refrigerator.

The syrup can be stored in the refrigerator for about a month.

Mexican Coffee Syrup

Ingredients

550 ml brown sugar

250 ml unsweetened cocoa powder

500 ml water

10 ml vanilla extract

1 whole clove

1 cinnamon stick

Method

Combine the sugar, water, cocoa powder, vanilla extract, clove and cinnamon stick together in a saucepan.

Heat the mixture until the sugar has dissolved.

Stir occasionally.

Reduce the heat once the sugar has dissolved and simmer for 15 minutes.

Remove the syrup from the heat.

Pour the syrup through a strainer to remove the solids.

Allow the syrup to cool and the store in the refrigerator.

The syrup can be stored in the refrigerator for about a month.

Mint Syrup

Ingredients

500 ml sugar

500 ml water

250 ml fresh mint leaves

Method

Combine the sugar, water and mint together in a saucepan.

Heat the mixture until the sugar has dissolved.

Stir occasionally.

Reduce the heat once the sugar has dissolved and simmer for 15 minutes.

Remove the syrup from the heat.

Pour the syrup through a strainer to remove the solids.

Allow the syrup to cool and the store in the refrigerator.

The syrup can be stored in the refrigerator for about a month.

Mocha Syrup

Ingredients

550 ml sugar

250 ml unsweetened cocoa powder

500 ml water

15 ml instant coffee granules

Method

Combine the sugar, water, cocoa powder and coffee together in a saucepan.

Heat the mixture until the sugar has dissolved.

Stir occasionally.

Reduce the heat once the sugar has dissolved and simmer for 15 minutes.

Remove the syrup from the heat.

Allow the syrup to cool and the store in the refrigerator.

The syrup can be stored in the refrigerator for about a month.

Orange Syrup

Ingredients

500 ml sugar

250 ml fresh orange juice

10 ml orange zest

25 ml lemon juice

25 ml corn syrup

50 ml Orange Liqueur

Method

Combine the sugar, orange juice, orange zest, lemon juice, corn syrup and Orange Liqueur together in a saucepan.

Heat the mixture until the sugar has dissolved.

Stir occasionally.

Reduce the heat once the sugar has dissolved and simmer for 15 minutes.

Remove the syrup from the heat.

Allow the syrup to cool and the store in the refrigerator.

The syrup can be stored in the refrigerator for about a month.

Peppermint Syrup

Ingredients

500 ml water

500 ml sugar

5 ml peppermint extract

Method

Combine the sugar, water and peppermint extract together in a saucepan.

Heat the mixture until the sugar has dissolved.

Stir occasionally.

Reduce the heat once the sugar has dissolved and simmer for 15 minutes.

Remove the syrup from the heat.

Allow the syrup to cool and the store in the refrigerator.

The syrup can be stored in the refrigerator for about a month.

Pumpkin Pie Syrup

Ingredients

500 ml sugar

500 ml water

10 ml ground cinnamon

15 ml pumpkin pie spice

2 ml ground cloves

Method

Combine the sugar, water, cinnamon, pumpkin pie spice and cloves together in a saucepan.

Heat the mixture until the sugar has dissolved.

Stir occasionally.

Reduce the heat once the sugar has dissolved and simmer for 15 minutes.

Remove the syrup from the heat.

Allow the syrup to cool and the store in the refrigerator.

The syrup can be stored in the refrigerator for about a month.

Raspberry Syrup

Ingredients

500 ml sugar

500 ml water

375 ml fresh raspberries

Method

Combine the sugar, water and raspberries together in a saucepan.

Heat the mixture until the sugar has dissolved.

Stir occasionally.

Reduce the heat once the sugar has dissolved and simmer for 15 minutes.

Remove the syrup from the heat.

Pour the syrup through a strainer to remove the solids.

Allow the syrup to cool and the store in the refrigerator.

The syrup can be stored in the refrigerator for about a month.

Rose Honey Syrup

Ingredients

500 ml sugar

500 ml water

125 ml rose petals

37,5 ml honey

Method

Combine the sugar, water, honey and rose petals together in a saucepan.

Heat the mixture until the sugar has dissolved.

Stir occasionally.

Reduce the heat once the sugar has dissolved and simmer for 15 minutes.

Remove the syrup from the heat.

Pour the syrup through a strainer to remove the solids.

Allow the syrup to cool and the store in the refrigerator.

The syrup can be stored in the refrigerator for about a month.

Rose Syrup

Ingredients

312 ml water

500 ml sugar

30 ml lime juice

62,5 ml rose water

Method

Combine the sugar, water, lime juice and rose water together in a saucepan.

Heat the mixture until the sugar has dissolved.

Stir occasionally.

Reduce the heat once the sugar has dissolved and simmer for 15 minutes.

Remove the syrup from the heat.

Allow the syrup to cool and the store in the refrigerator.

The syrup can be stored in the refrigerator for about a month.

Saffron Honey Syrup

Ingredients

500 ml sugar

500 ml water

50 ml honey

2 ml saffron threads (packed)

1 cinnamon stick

1 star anise

1 whole clove

Method

Combine the sugar, water, honey, saffron threads, cinnamon stick, star anise and clove together in a saucepan.

Heat the mixture until the sugar has dissolved.

Stir occasionally.

Reduce the heat once the sugar has dissolved and simmer for 15 minutes.

Remove the syrup from the heat.

Pour the syrup through a strainer to remove the solids.

Allow the syrup to cool and the store in the refrigerator.

The syrup can be stored in the refrigerator for about a month.

Saffron Syrup

Ingredients

500 ml sugar

500 ml water

1 vanilla bean (split lengthwise – scrape seeds out of pod)

5 ml saffron threads (firmly packed)

20 ml lemon zest

Method

Combine the sugar, water, vanilla seeds, vanilla pod, lemon zest and saffron threads together in a saucepan.

Heat the mixture until the sugar has dissolved.

Stir occasionally.

Reduce the heat once the sugar has dissolved and simmer for 15 minutes.

Remove the syrup from the heat.

Remove the vanilla pod.

Allow the syrup to cool and the store in the refrigerator.

The syrup can be stored in the refrigerator for about a month.

Strawberry Syrup

Ingredients

500 ml sugar

500 ml water

375 ml fresh strawberries

Method

Combine the sugar, water and strawberries together in a saucepan.

Heat the mixture until the sugar has dissolved.

Stir occasionally.

Reduce the heat once the sugar has dissolved and simmer for 15 minutes.

Remove the syrup from the heat.

Pour the syrup through a strainer to remove the solids.

Allow the syrup to cool and the store in the refrigerator.

The syrup can be stored in the refrigerator for about a month.

Turkish Coffee Syrup

Ingredients

500 ml sugar

500 ml strong black coffee

10 rose water

Method

Combine the sugar, coffee and rose water together in a saucepan.

Heat the mixture until the sugar has dissolved.

Stir occasionally.

Reduce the heat once the sugar has dissolved and simmer for 15 minutes.

Remove the syrup from the heat.

Allow the syrup to cool and the store in the refrigerator.

The syrup can be stored in the refrigerator for about a month.

Vanilla Syrup

Ingredients

500 ml sugar

500 ml water

1 vanilla bean (split lengthwise – scrape seeds out of pod)

5 ml vanilla extract

Method

Combine the sugar, water, vanilla seeds and vanilla pod together in a saucepan.

Heat the mixture until the sugar has dissolved.

Stir occasionally.

Reduce the heat once the sugar has dissolved and simmer for 15 minutes.

Remove the syrup from the heat.

Remove the vanilla pod.

Add the vanilla extract.

Allow the syrup to cool and the store in the refrigerator.

The syrup can be stored in the refrigerator for about a month.

Made in United States
Troutdale, OR
12/17/2024